FIRST 50
GUITAR DUETS

YOU SHOULD PLAY

Arranged by Mark Phillips

All music can be played with pick or fingers; however, for non-adjacent strings use
fingers or hybrid picking (pick and fingers simultaneously).

ISBN 978-1-5400-6812-5

HAL•LEONARD®

Visit Hal Leonard Online at
www.halleonard.com

Contact Us:
Hal Leonard
7777 West Bluemound Road
Milwaukee, WI 53213
Email: info@halleonard.com

In Europe, contact:
Hal Leonard Europe Limited
42 Wigmore Street
Marylebone, London, W1U 2RN
Email: info@halleonardeurope.com

In Australia, contact:
Hal Leonard Australia Pty. Ltd.
4 Lentara Court
Cheltenham, Victoria, 3192 Australia
Email: info@halleonard.com.au

GUITAR NOTATION LEGEND

THE MUSICAL STAFF shows pitches and rhythms and is divided by bar lines into measures. Pitches are named after the first seven letters of the alphabet.

TABLATURE graphically represents the guitar fingerboard. Each horizontal line represents a string, and each number represents a fret.

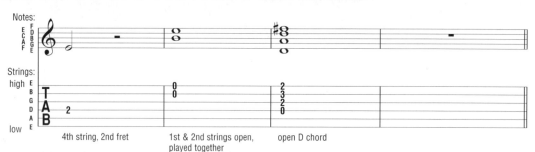

4th string, 2nd fret

1st & 2nd strings open, played together

open D chord

HALF-STEP BEND: Strike the note and bend up 1/2 step.

WHOLE-STEP BEND: Strike the note and bend up one step.

GRACE NOTE BEND: Strike the note and immediately bend up as indicated.

SLIGHT (MICROTONE) BEND: Strike the note and bend up 1/4 step.

BEND AND RELEASE: Strike the note and bend up as indicated, then release back to the original note. Only the first note is struck.

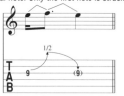

PRE-BEND: Bend the note as indicated, then strike it.

VIBRATO: The string is vibrated by rapidly bending and releasing the note with the fretting hand.

PALM MUTING: The note is partially muted by the pick hand lightly touching the string(s) just before the bridge.

HAMMER-ON: Strike the first (lower) note with one finger, then sound the higher note (on the same string) with another finger by fretting it without picking.

PULL-OFF: Place both fingers on the notes to be sounded. Strike the first note and without picking, pull the finger off to sound the second (lower) note.

LEGATO SLIDE: Strike the first note and then slide the same fret-hand finger up or down to the second note. The second note is not struck.

SHIFT SLIDE: Same as legato slide, except the second note is struck.

TRILL: Very rapidly alternate between the notes indicated by continuously hammering on and pulling off.

TAPPING: Hammer ("tap") the fret indicated with the pick-hand index or middle finger and pull off to the note fretted by the fret hand.

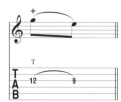

NATURAL HARMONIC: Strike the note while the fret-hand lightly touches the string directly over the fret indicated.

PINCH HARMONIC: The note is fretted normally and a harmonic is produced by adding the edge of the thumb or the tip of the index finger of the pick hand to the normal pick attack.

TREMOLO PICKING: The note is picked as rapidly and continuously as possible.

VIBRATO BAR DIVE AND RETURN: The pitch of the note or chord is dropped a specified number of steps (in rhythm), then returned to the original pitch.

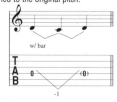

VIBRATO BAR SCOOP: Depress the bar just before striking the note, then quickly release the bar.

VIBRATO BAR DIP: Strike the note and then immediately drop a specified number of steps, then release back to the original pitch.

Additional Musical Definitions

(accent)

- Accentuate note (play it louder).

(staccato)

- Play the note short.

D.S. al Coda

- Go back to the sign (%), then play until the measure marked "*To Coda*," then skip to the section labelled "**Coda**."

D.C. al Fine

- Go back to the beginning of the song and play until the measure marked "*Fine*" (end).

Fill

N.C.

- Label used to identify a brief melodic figure which is to be inserted into the arrangement.

- Harmony is implied.

- Repeat measures between signs.

- When a repeated section has different endings, play the first ending only the first time and the second ending only the second time.

CONTENTS

Autumn Leaves

English lyric by Johnny Mercer
French lyric by Jacques Prevert
Music by Joseph Kosma

Bridge Over Troubled Water

Words and Music by Paul Simon

D.S. al Coda

Ⓞ **Coda**

rit.

Brown Eyed Girl

Words and Music by Van Morrison

Moderately fast

Can You Feel
the Love Tonight

from THE LION KING

Music by Elton John
Lyrics by Tim Rice

Can't Help Falling in Love

from the Paramount Picture BLUE HAWAII

Words and Music by George David Weiss, Hugo Peretti and Luigi Creatore

Candle in the Wind

Words and Music by Elton John and Bernie Taupin

Chim Chim Cher-ee

from MARY POPPINS
Words and Music by Richard M. Sherman and Robert B. Sherman

Chopsticks

By Arthur de Lulli

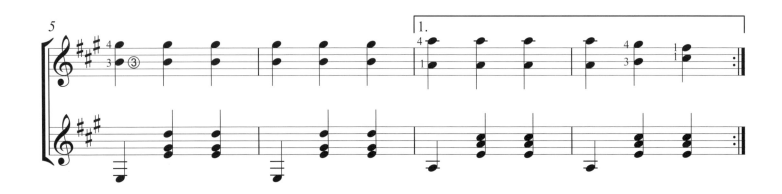

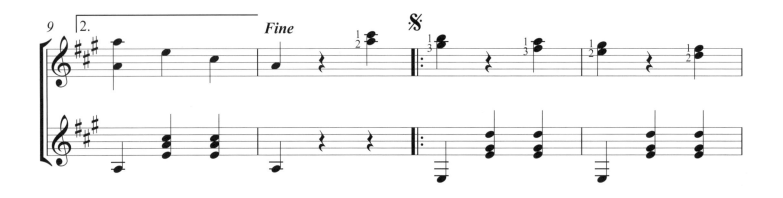

Climb Ev'ry Mountain

from THE SOUND OF MUSIC

Lyrics by Oscar Hammerstein II
Music by Richard Rodgers

Clocks

Words and Music by Guy Berryman, Jon Buckland, Will Champion and Chris Martin

Gtr. II: Drop D tuning:
(low to high) D-A-D-G-B-E

Moderately

Eleanor Rigby

Words and Music by John Lennon and Paul McCartney

Moderately fast

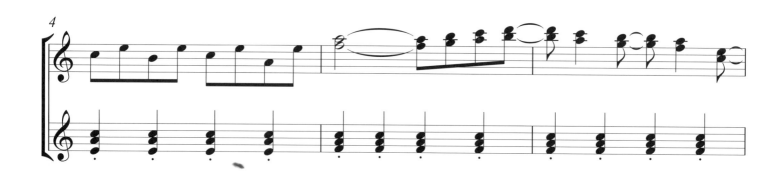

Every Breath You Take

Music and Lyrics by Sting

D.S. al Coda

Coda

Sweet Baby James

Words and Music by James Taylor

*Strum

sim.

31

Fly Me to the Moon
(In Other Words)

Words and Music by Bart Howard

Game of Thrones

Theme from the HBO Series GAME OF THRONES

By Ramin Djawadi

Moderately fast, in 2

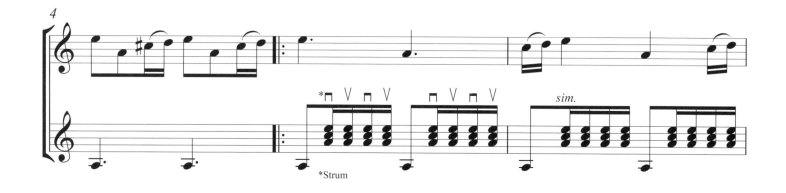

God Bless America®

Words and Music by Irving Berlin

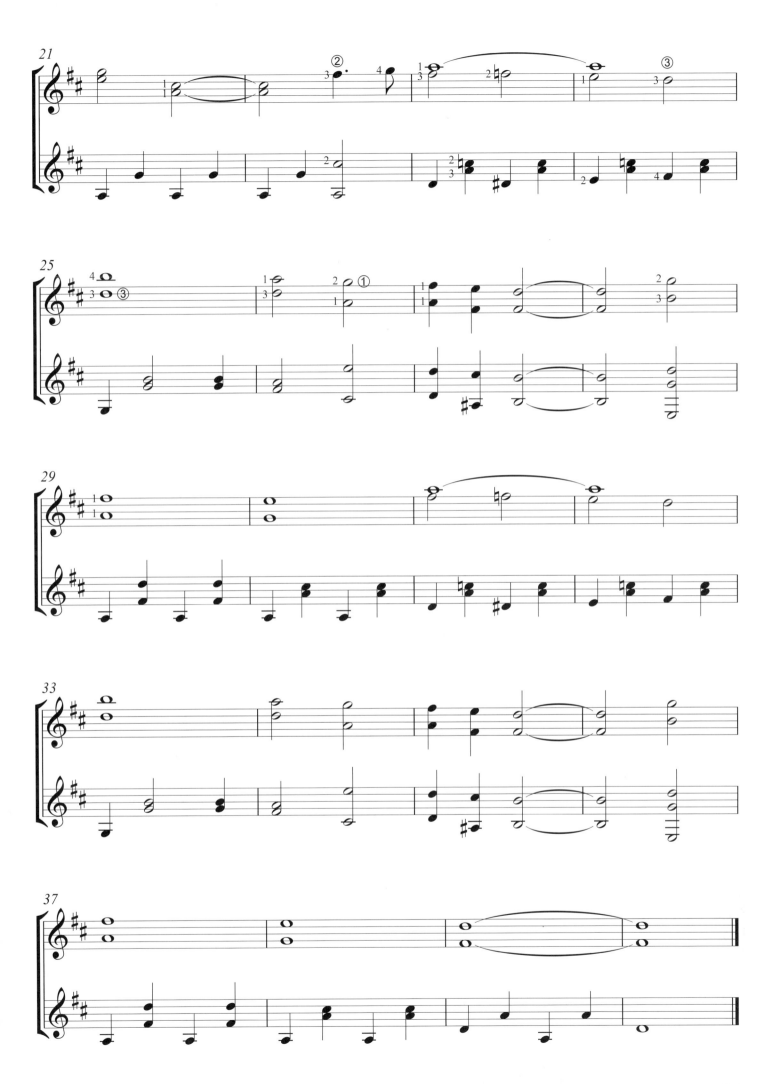

God Only Knows

Words and Music by Brian Wilson and Tony Asher

Goldfinger

from GOLDFINGER

Music by John Barry
Lyrics by Leslie Bricusse and Anthony Newley

Hallelujah

Words and Music by Leonard Cohen

Heart and Soul

from the Paramount Short Subject A SONG IS BORN

Words by Frank Loesser
Music by Hoagy Carmichael

Human Nature

Words and Music by John Bettis and Steve Porcaro

Hurt

Words and Music by Trent Reznor

Imagine

Words and Music by John Lennon

Moderately slow

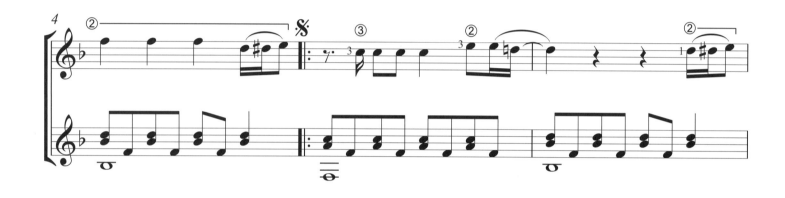

*Continue fingering in 3rd postion till otherwise indicated.

*Continue fingering in 5th postion till otherwise indicated.

In My Life

Words and Music by John Lennon and Paul McCartney

Lean on Me

Words and Music by Bill Withers

Let It Go

from FROZEN

Music and Lyrics by Kristen Anderson-Lopez and Robert Lopez

Linus and Lucy

from A CHARLIE BROWN CHRISTMAS
By Vince Guaraldi

Gtr. II: Drop D tuning:
(low to high) D-A-D-G-B-E

Memory
from CATS

Music by Andrew Lloyd Webber
Text by Trevor Nunn after T.S. Eliot

D.S. al Coda

Coda

Michelle

Words and Music by John Lennon and Paul McCartney

Mission: Impossible Theme

from the Paramount Television Series MISSION: IMPOSSIBLE

By Lalo Schifrin

Gtr. II: Drop D tuning:
(low to high) D-A-D-G-B-E

Fast

Moon River

from the Paramount Picture BREAKFAST AT TIFFANY'S

Words by Johnny Mercer
Music by Henry Mancini

My Cherie Amour

Words and Music by Stevie Wonder, Sylvia Moy and Henry Cosby

Gtr. II: Drop D tuning:
(low to high) D-A-D-G-B-E

Moderately

My Funny Valentine

from BABES IN ARMS
Words by Lorenz Hart
Music by Richard Rodgers

Over the Rainbow

from THE WIZARD OF OZ
Music by Harold Arlen
Lyric by E.Y. "Yip" Harburg

Peter Gunn
Theme Song from the Television Series
By Henry Mancini

The Rainbow Connection

from THE MUPPET MOVIE

Words and Music by Paul Williams and Kenneth L. Ascher

Seven Nation Army

Words and Music by Jack White

Shape of You

Words and Music by Ed Sheeran, Kevin Briggs, Kandi Burruss,
Tameka Cottle, Steve Mac and Johnny McDaid

Moderately, in 2

Sleepwalk
(Instrumental Version)

By Santo Farina, John Farina and Ann Farina

Stand by Me

Words and Music by Jerry Leiber, Mike Stoller and Ben E. King

Star Wars
(Main Theme)

from STAR WARS: A NEW HOPE

Music by John Williams

Summertime

from PORGY AND BESS®

Music and Lyrics by George Gershwin, DuBose and Dorothy Heyward and Ira Gershwin

Sunrise, Sunset

from the Musical FIDDLER ON THE ROOF

Words by Sheldon Harnick
Music by Jerry Bock

Gtr. II: Drop D tuning:
(low to high) D-A-D-G-B-E

Sway
(Quien Será)

English Words by Norman Gimbel
Spanish Words and Music by Pablo Beltran Ruiz and Luis Demetrio Traconis Molina

Time in a Bottle

Words and Music by Jim Croce

Tomorrow

from the Musical Production ANNIE

Lyric by Martin Charnin
Music by Charles Strouse

Gtr. II: Drop D tuning:
(low to high) D-A-D-G-B-E

Moderately slow

When I Fall in Love

from ONE MINUTE TO ZERO

Words by Edward Heyman
Music by Victor Young

Moderately slow

With or Without You

Words and Music by U2

You Raise Me Up

Words and Music by Brendan Graham and Rolf Lovland

Gtr. II: Drop D tuning:
(low to high) D-A-D-G-B-E

What a Wonderful World

Words and Music by George David Weiss and Bob Thiele